# BOEING B-52 STRATOFORTRESS

## 2ND EDITION

# BOEING B-52 STRATOFORTRESS

## 2ND EDITION

**WILLIAM HOLDER AND
ROBERT WOODSIDE**

*AERO*
A division of TAB BOOKS Inc.
Blue Ridge Summit, PA

*Aero* series

34

SECOND EDITION
FIRST PRINTING

Copyright © 1988 by TAB BOOKS Inc.
Printed in the United States of America

Library of Congress Cataloging in Publication Data

Holder, William G., 1937-
Boeing B-52 Stratofortress / by William Holder and Robert
Woodside.
p.   cm. — (Aero series ; vol. 34)
Includes index.
ISBN 0-8306-8615-0 (pbk.)
1. B-52 Bomber.  I. Woodside, Robert. II. Title.
UG1242.B6H64   1988                         87-35151
623.74'63—dc19                                   CIP

Questions regarding the content of this book
should be addressed to:

Reader Inquiry Branch
TAB BOOKS Inc.
Blue Ridge Summit, PA  17294-0214

# Contents

# Foreword

Here is the copiously illustrated story of the airplane that some observers believe history will characterize as the single most important military aircraft ever possessed by the United States, the Boeing B-52 Stratofortress. This new, second edition brings the B-52's service history up-to-date.

For more than three decades the B-52 global bomber has constituted the vital third leg of America's nuclear deterrent triad. Along with atomic attack submarines and intercontinental ballastic missiles, the Big Ugly Fat Fellow ("BUFF" to its crews) has been a major factor in the enforcement of a peaceful coexistence with the Soviets.

Regarded by the Air Force as at least 10 years ahead of its time when it entered service in the 1950s, this unique behemoth of an airplane was so well conceived that, given more powerful engines, increasingly sophisticated avionics, and electronic countermeasures systems, it has kept pace with its ever more difficult mission; and despite development of the supersonic B-1B and Stealth nuclear bombers, the last of the more than 700 B-52s built is not expected to face retirement until early in the 21st century.

Currently armed with a mix of nuclear bombs and nuclear-tipped SRAMs or cruise missiles, America's B-52 fleet remains a credible, and most visible, retaliatory force that provides the flexibility necessary to ensure against accidental war. The manned bomber may be launched at the earliest—perhaps uncertain—indication that hostilities have been initiated by the other side. Then, for hours afterwards, it may be recalled if necessary.

The BUFF's mission profiles, which have necessarily changed with the times, are described here, along with its operating systems and flight characteristics. Military aircraft enthusiasts will find this an accurate and detailed portrayal of this very significant aircraft.

JOE CHRISTY

# Acknowledgments

The authors wish to thank the following individuals and organizations for their assistance in the preparation of this book:

Office of Public Affairs,
Aeronautical Systems Division,
Wright-Patterson Air Force Base

Research Staff,
Air Force Museum,
Wright-Patterson Air Force Base

The Boeing Company

Special thanks to Glenn Holder for editing the final manuscript.

# 1
# Genealogy

SOMETHING BIG WAS IN THE AIR! THE BUSY FLIGHT RAMP AT Anderson Air Force Base in Guam was abuzz. Maintenance crews sweated over their giant bombers, checking every nut and bolt. Bombs were loaded internally into the Stratoforts' massive bomb bays on preloaded bomb racks. Twenty-four bombs on the external wing racks were hung one at a time. It was December 1972, and the B-52 was going to face its toughest challenge ever—LINEBACKER II was on!

The flight crews heard the news three hours before takeoff on that first day—''Gentlemen, we are going to strike targets in the Hanoi-Haiphong area.'' Weather—''it's bad;'' enemy defenses—''tough;'' order of battle—''max effort.'' The B-52s had been saturation bombing in South Vietnam for years, basically unmolested, but this would be the first maximum effort ''up north.'' The crews knew it would be tough going.

The B-52s pounded North Vietnam for eleven days, during which time the enemy launched more than 1,000 surface-to-air missiles (SAMs) against the fleet. Many times the missiles came up in salvos of two or four. And when the SAMs got through, the MIGs were waiting. For those bloody and heroic days, the skies over North Vietnam were alive with bursting SAMs, flashing rockets, and falling, burning airplanes—a good number of which were the giant Stratoforts. During the operation the B-52s flew some 700 sorties.

The losses of LINEBACKER II were high—many felt that they were too high. Twenty-six aircraft were lost, of which 15 were B-52s. Actually the loss amounted to two percent of the B-52s involved. But the giant Stratoforts did the job! And with the termination of LINEBACKER II, the Southeast Asian conflict ground to its eventual stand-down. The B-52 had proved in Vietnam what the B-17 and B-29 had proved in World War II, that is, the total devastation of the enemy homeland with conventional ordnance can be the winning hand for stopping hostilities. The giant B-52 with 108 "iron bombs" was indeed a devastating weapon. But the bird was, in effect, playing a role for which it had never been cast. Conceived in the time of nuclear-weapon infancy and the climate of the Cold War, the B-52 had been envisioned as a high-altitude carrier of nuclear destruction. Its conversion to an iron-bomb hauler is only one of the many transitions this amazing and versatile aircraft has made during its lifetime.

The B-52's genealogical roots go deep. As early as 1945, the Army Air Force discussed the possibilities and characteristics for new postwar bombers. By November of that year, firm characteristics for a high-speed, high-altitude, long-range bomber had been formulated. The requirements called for a plane capable of "carrying 10,000 pounds of bombs for 5,000 miles while operating at a speed of 300 MPH at 35,000 feet."

Proposals for the new aircraft were submitted by Martin, Consolidated Vultee, and Boeing. The Consolidated Vultee entry evolved into the XB-60 bomber, which was basically a swept-wing, jet-powered version of its B-36.

Boeing submitted a design, the Model 462, for a six-engined aircraft weighing 360,000 pounds with a 3,100-mile radius and a 410-MPH cruising speed. The straight-wing design, which bore a marked similarity to the previous B-29, featured a nosewheel undercarriage arrangement which retracted into the engine nacelle. However, the Air Force Air Materiel Command's concern about the model's extremely high gross weight caused several alternate configurations to be examined.

During discussions of new medium bombers, Boeing presented Design Study 464, which outlined a four-engine aircraft with a gross weight of 230,000 pounds and a 400-MPH cruising speed. In 1946, plans were formulated for a four-engine aircraft with a 12,000-mile range, a 400-MPH cruising speed, and the capability of carrying nuclear weapons. Studies by Boeing resulted in two designs differing only in bomb load capabilities. The Model 464-16 carried only 10,000 pounds, whereas the general-purpose Model 464-17 had a bomb bay capacity of 90,000 pounds. Work was started on the -17 design but was halted in June 1947 when new heavy-bomber requirements were formulated.

With in-flight refueling a reality, the planner's attentions turned to an aircraft with greater speed capability. An improved model evolved from Boeing drawing boards as the Model 464-29, which featured more sharply tapered wings with a 20-degree sweep. Grossing out at about 400,000 pounds, the craft would achieve a maximum speed of almost 450 MPH. Several other turboprop models were also considered, including the Model 464-35, which promised a top speed of 500 MPH. For almost three years, the bomber configuration studies had floundered through a series of changing requirements and revisions. The Boeing designs during that time period had closely resembled the company's B-17, B-29, and B-50 forefathers. The new bomber would replace the B-36, yet the turboprop propulsion of the early Boeing designs provided only minimal advantages over the B-36.

In May of 1948, Boeing was requested to expand its performance studies and include configuration studies using pure jet power for the first time, and with rapidly-improving jet engine technology, the engineers felt that the pure jet was the only way to go. Boeing's highly-successful experimental flights of the six-engine B-47 jet confirmed the high speed and comparative simplicity of jet engines. The troublesome fuel consumption problems of jets appeared to be solved.

It was, therefore, not surprising that the design for Model 464-40 was born with strictly jet engines (Westinghouse J-40s). The 464-40 incorporated a minimum of changes from the turboprop version, with no increase in liftoff weight. Models 464-46 and -47 were further refinements of the -40 configuration and would use the new Pratt and Whitney J57 engine.

With the advent of Model 464-49, the new bomber was finally starting to look like the B-52. But in other respects, it also looked much like a scaled-up B-47, also under development at that time. The new design incorporated eight J57 engines, possessed additional fuel capacity, and carried only one turret instead of the previous two, but the new machine showed a 50,000-pound increase in gross weight. It didn't take long, however, for the Air Force brass to decide that this indeed was the giant bird that it had been looking for. The XB-52 would be an eight-jet, swept-wing creation.

From a performance standpoint, the design possessed some outstanding flight characteristics. It was to have a design gross weight of some 330,000 pounds, a range of 8,000 miles, and demonstrate a top speed of an impressive 572 MPH. The plane's bombing altitude was assessed as 45,000 feet.

During the evolutionary process to the Model 464-49, and the slightly-refined Model 464-201, there was great skepticism as to whether the revolutionary new plane would fly. The old propeller-powered, straight-wing school still had deep roots and rejected change. Armament and landing-gear weight also generated many arguments during the design stages. For a time the idea of dropping certain outboard landing-gear components after takeoff (to reduce the gross weight), was considered. Arguments about crew size raged with some configurations having as many as 15 on station.

The five-or-so years of B-52 definition had seen a tremendous evolutionary process take place. In fact, it could well be defined as a move from the straight-wing technology of World War II to the swept-wing jet era. Speed capability increased from 382 knots to 490 knots on the final configuration. But gross weight remained nearly constant—about 400,000 pounds.

Finally, the time for metal cutting arrived. There would be two prototypes, coined the XB-52 and the YB-52. The XB-52 was the first, grossing out at about 390,000 pounds. Resembling a scaled-up B-47, the XB-52 sported a 35-degree sweep and eight (two per pod) J57 turbojets. The aircraft also had two four-wheel fuselage-mounted main landing gear which possessed a unique crosswind capability. Wingtip-mounted wheels were required because of wing droop with a full fuel load. The XB-52 also carried a large braking parachute in the tail compartment. The B-47 influence on these early prototypes was also evident by their tandem seating arrangement for the pilot and co-pilot. Production Stratoforts, however, would adopt the familiar side-by-side seating.

The Air Force knew it really had something with its new superbomber, and a tight cloak of secrecy covered its development. Early photographs showed the new aircraft covered with concealing tarps much like new-model cars.

Extensive modifications to the XB-52 were required before it was ready for its first flight on October 2, 1952. This delay allowed the second prototype, the YB-52, to make its first flight in advance of the XB-52. On September 4, 1954, the YB-52 made a Seattle-to-Dayton run at a speed of 624 MPH, performing better than the jet fighters of the Bendix Trophy Race from California to Dayton.

The flight tests of the X and Y prototypes proved that the Stratofort was ready. It was finally time to get the production lines rolling.

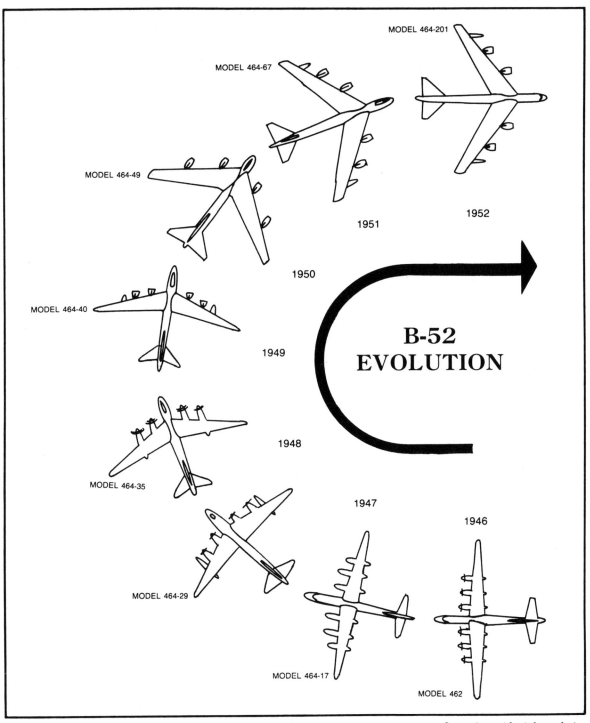

MODEL 464-201

MODEL 464-67

MODEL 464-49

1952

1951

MODEL 464-40

1950

1949

MODEL 464-35

1948

B-52
EVOLUTION

1947

1946

MODEL 464-29

MODEL 464-17

MODEL 462

*The evolution of the B-52 design: from a straight-wing six-prop design to a swept-wing configuration with eight turbojet engines (two per pod). It all occurred in the six years following World War II. (from a Stallman Illustration)*

*A sign of the times before the giant B-52 bombers started to roam the skies. Here, a B-47 takes on a load of fuel from a KC-97 prop-powered tanker. (courtesy U.S. Air Force)*

*The B-52 made the B-47 obsolete for many missions. Many B-47s were retired in the late 1960s and mothballed at Davis-Monthan Air Force Base. (courtesy U.S. Air Force)*

*Looking much like a B-47 with eight engines instead of six, the XB-52 made one of its virgin flights. (courtesy Boeing)*

*The XB-52's cockpit seating was a tandem arrangement. The YB-52 featured the side-by-side seating that was used on all the remaining models. (courtesy Boeing)*

*The YB-52 in one of its early test flights. Although this aircraft was built after the XB, it was the earlier of the two to fly. (courtesy Boeing)*

*Another aircraft that was built during the period was the B-58 Hustler bomber. Fewer than a hundred were constructed. They served for only a short period of time before being stored and eventually destroyed. Only two remain today. (courtesy U.S. Air Force)*

# 2

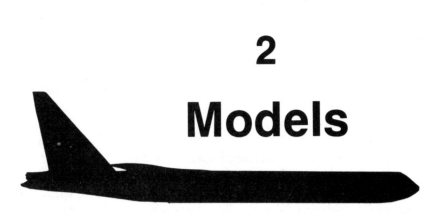

# Models

FOR ELEVEN YEARS AND THROUGH SEVEN DIFFERENT MODELS the B-52 production lines hummed. In all, 742 Stratofortresses were produced of which 275 were built at Boeing's Seattle facility. But the bulk of the production program, 467 aircraft (including all the later models), were produced at Boeing's giant Wichita plant.

The B-52 program started on sounder footing than any other large aircraft program. In fact, the Air Force authorized production tooling contracts ahead of the actual production contracts. Only one other new aircraft in U.S. aviation history had earned similar confidence prior to its first flight—the B-29.

The B-52A maintained a basic similarity to the XB and YB prototypes. The most noticeable changes were a four-foot longer nose and elimination of the B-47-type bubble canopy. Carrying a crew of six, the A models were equipped with J57-P-1W powerplants and grossed out at about 420,000 pounds. Carrying two 1,000-pound drop tanks, the B-52A could turn 490 knots at over 46,000 feet.

The initial B-52A rolled out of the Seattle plant on March 18, 1954 and made its first flight test on August 5, 1954. Only three A-model Stratoforts were built and they never saw operational SAC service, but were later used for basic testing.

On January 25, 1955, the first B-52B took to the air from Seattle. The B-model was the first Stratofort to be delivered to SAC (specifically, the 93rd Bomb Wing) and incorporated several changes, including the MA-6A bombing navigation system. The B-52B was the version that set the first of many significant B-52 range and endurance records. Three B-52Bs, flying at an average speed of 452 knots, completed a round-the-world trip on January 18, 1957, in 45 hours, 19 minutes.

RB-52B was the designation given to those -52B's with reconnaissance capability. Twenty-seven of that special variant were built.

March 9, 1956 saw the first flight of the B-52C—the last pure Seattle-produced Stratofort. The B-52C had larger underwing drop tanks and its all-up weight increased to 450,000 pounds. Thirty-five were built.

With the advent of the D model, the B-52 also began production at Wichita, although 101 of the 170 B-52Ds that were produced were built at Seattle. The Seattle Stratoforts were built concurrently with the KC-135A tanker-transports. The first B-52D test flight occurred at Seattle on September 28, 1956, and the B-52D later underwent significant modifications for Vietnam operations.

Exactly 100 B-52E aircraft were built, with Wichita assuming production leadership by building 58. The first B-52E flight took place at Seattle on October 3, 1957, and the initial Wichita flight came two weeks later. The B-52E was the first of the breed to carry the Hound Dog air-to-surface missile, along with improved bombing, navigation, and electronics systems.

The last Seattle-produced B-52 was the F model, giving Seattle a total Stratofort production output of 275 aircraft. The B-52F was equipped with so-called ''hard-drive'' alternators, which were connected to the port unit of each pair of jet engines.

Wichita produced 193 B-52Gs, with the first aircraft coming off the line on October 17, 1958. It was the highest number of any model produced. The G variant incorporated extensive changes with a redesigned wing containing internal fuel tanks. The fuel capacity was increased to a whopping 46,000 gallons, pushing its gross weight to 488,000 pounds. A significant tactical change had the gunner positioned in the pressurized forward portion of the aircraft, while a TV camera replaced the gunner in the tail. The B-52G demonstrated 25-percent greater range, increased climb performance, and greater over-target altitude. To demonstrate its improved capability, a manned Air Force B-52G landed at Edwards Air Force Base, California, to complete a 28-hour, non-stop flight of almost 13,000 miles. But the most noticeable outward change was the shortening of the vertical fin, a change which would be carried through to the final H version.

The B-52G actually entered SAC service in February 1959. A B-52G, fitted with turbofan engines and serving as a flying test bed for the H model, flew for the first time in July 1960.

The B-52H was the last of the Stratoforts, with Wichita turning out 102 of the model between September 1960 and October 1962. The B-52H, equipped with Pratt and Whitney TF-33 turbofans, was a radical improvement over its earlier brothers. The advanced powerplants gave the B-52H a 10 to 15 percent increase in range and made the H model seem like an entirely new airplane. An operational B-52H demonstrated the improved capability with a 12,500-mile non-stop trip from Okinawa to Madrid in less than 22 hours to set or break 11 distance, course, and speed records without refueling. Another -52H advancement was the substitution of the 6,000-round-per-minute, six-barrel Gatling gun for the original four-gun tail-turret.

Although the B-52G and B-52H are very similar in appearance, they differ greatly internally. In addition to the improved powerplants, the initial H model offered advanced low-altitude capabilities and additional crew comfort provisions for long-duration flights. The B-52H was the last production version of the Stratofort.

In 1975, the Joint Strategic Bomber Study examined the then-new B-1 and three other aircraft alternatives—a stretched FB-111, a stand-off cruise-missile-launching aircraft similar to the Boeing 747, and finally a re-engined Stratofort, the B-52I. The B-52I was to be a four-engined B-52, but the version never went beyond the concept phase. The I version would have incorporated much more powerful engines and new electronics technology. The program was not to be a new production effort, just a modification of the G and H fleet. The age of the B-52 airframes, plus the cost of the extensive modification, were the main reasons the rework was not accomplished.

Six years later, Pratt and Whitney proposed that the G model could be re-engined with the PW2037 turbofan engine (once again, four of them), which was being developed for the Boeing 757 commercial airliner and the McDonnell Douglas C-17 cargo aircraft. The cost of re-engining the complete B-52G fleet (which numbered 173 aircraft at the time) was estimated at $4.2 billion. The main benefit of the proposed project, according to the manufacturer, was increased fuel efficiency—each aircraft would supposedly burn about 700,000 fewer gallons of fuel annually. The increased thrust capability of the proposed configuration would also have reduced the takeoff roll by some 1,500 feet. But alas, the attractive proposition was never adopted, and the B-52G fleet remained unchanged.

In 1987, the idea of re-engining the remaining 167 B-52Gs popped up again as a Boeing proposal. The study centered on replacing the eight existing engines with four turbofans—either the Rolls-Royce 535E4 or the Pratt & Whitney PW2037. As of this writing, no decision had been made concerning the proposed modification.

Then too, there is also no firm determination on the final use of the B-52G fleet. There has been a proposal to modify the G models to carry standoff conventional munitions.

| | | | B-52 Major Model Differences | | |
|---|---|---|---|---|---|

| MODEL | AF SERIAL NO. | A/P PROD. NO. | INITIAL DELIVERY | FIRE CONTROL SYSTEM | BOMB NAV. SYSTEM |
|---|---|---|---|---|---|
| **XB-52** | 49-230 | 1 (Prototype) | Apr. 1953 | None | None |
| **YB-52** | 49-231 | 1 (Prototype) | Mar. 1953 | | |
| **B-52A** | 52-001 thru 52-003 | 1-3 | Jun. 1954 | A-3A | None |
| **B-52B** | 52-004 thru 52-013<br>52-8710 thru 52-8716<br>53-366 thru 53-376<br>53-377 thru 53-391<br>53-392 thru 53-398 | 4-13<br>14-20<br>21-31<br>32-46<br>47-53 | Sep. 1954<br>Jun. 1955<br>Aug. 1955<br>Nov. 1955<br>Feb. 1956 | A-3A<br>MD-5<br>MD-5<br>MD-5<br>A-3A | MA-6A<br>MA-6A<br>MA-6A<br>MA-6A<br>MA-6A |
| **B-52C** | 53-399 thru 53-408<br>53-2664 thru 53-2688 | 54-63<br>64-88 | Apr. 1956<br>Jun. 1956 | A-3A | AN/ASQ-48(V)<br>AN/ASB-15<br>AN/APN-108<br>MD-1 |
| **B-52D** Seattle | 55-068 thru 55-117<br>56-580 thru 56-630 | 89-138<br>139-189 | Oct. 1956<br>Apr. 1957 | MD-9 | |
| **B-52D** Wichita | 55-049 thru 55-067<br>55-673 thru 55-680<br>56-657 thru 56-698 | 1-19<br>20-27<br>28-69 | Jun. 1956<br>Mar. 1957<br>Jun. 1957 | | |
| **B-52E** Seattle | 56-631 thru 56-656<br>57-014 thru 57-029 | 190-215<br>216-231 | Nov. 1957<br>Feb. 1958 | MD-9 | AN/ASQ-38(V)<br>AN/ASB-4A<br>AN/APN-89A<br>MD-1, AJA-1 |
| **B-52E** Wichita | 56-699 thru 56-712<br>57-095 thru 57-138 | 70-83<br>84-127 | Nov. 1957<br>Dec. 1957 | | |
| **B-52F** Seattle | 57-030 thru 57-073 | 232-275 | May 1958 | MD-9 | AN/ASQ-38(V)<br>AN/ASB-4A<br>AN/APN-89A<br>MD-1, AJA-1 |
| **B-52F** Wichita | 57-139 thru 57-183 | 128-172 | Jun. 1958 | | |
| **B-52G** Wichita | 57-6468 thru 57-6520<br>58-158 thru 58-258<br>59-2564 thru 59-2602 | 173-225<br>226-326<br>327-365 | Oct. 1958<br>Jul. 1959<br>Jun. 1960 | AN/ASG-15 | AN/ASQ-38(V)<br>AN/ASB-16<br>AN/APN-89A<br>MD-1,AJA-1 |
| **B-52H** Wichita | 60-001 & On | 366 & On | Mar. 1961 | AN/ASG-21 | AN/ASQ-38(V)<br>AN/ASB-9A<br>AN/APN-89A<br>MD-1, AJN-8<br>J-4 |

| ENGINES | EXTERNAL DROP TANKS GALS. | MAXIMUM GROSS WT. LBS. | OPERATING WT. EMPTY LBS. | FUEL CAPACITY |
|---|---|---|---|---|
| 4 J57-P-38<br>2 J75 | 1,000 | 405,000 | | 38,865 |
| J57-P-3 | | | | |
| J57-P-1W | 1,000 | 420,000 | 167,509 | 37,550 |
| J57-P-1W<br>J57-P-29W or<br>J57-P-29WA or<br>J57-P-19W | 1,000 | 420,000 | 169,599 | 37,550 |
| J57-P-29WA or<br>J57-P-19W | 3,000 | 450,000 | 170,745 | 41,550 |
| J57-P-29W or<br>J57-P-19W | 3,000 | 450,000 | 171,666 | 41,550 |
| J57-P-29W or<br>J57-P-19W | 3,000 | 450,000 | 172,602 | 41,550 |
| J57-P-43W or<br>J57-P-43WA or<br>J57-P-43WB | 3,000 | 450,000 | 170,228 | 41,550 |
| J57-P-43W or<br>J57-P-43WB | 700 (Fixed) | 488,000<br>(525,000<br>in-flight) | 164,091 | 47,975<br>(Integral Fuel<br>Wing) |
| TF33-P-3 | 700 (Fixed) | 488,000<br>(525,000<br>in-flight) | 165,466 | 47,975<br>(Integral Fuel<br>Wing) |

## B-52 CONSTRUCTION CHRONOLOGY

1946   *JANUARY:* Air Force sets up basic requirements for new bomber.
       *JUNE:* Boeing awarded engineering study and preliminary design contract for new bomber.

1947   *SEPTEMBER 30:* First public announcement of B-52.

1951   *MARCH 15:* Boeing received Air Force "Letter of Intent" for B-52 production tooling.
       *NOVEMBER 29:* Rollout of XB-52.

1952   *MARCH 15:* Rollout of YB-52.
       *APRIL 15:* First flight of YB-52.
       *OCTOBER 2:* First flight of XB-52.

1953   *SEPTEMBER 28:* Wichita named as second source for B-52 production.

1954   *MARCH 18:* First B-52A rollout.
       *AUGUST 5:* First flight of B-52A at Seattle.

1955   *JANUARY 25:* First flight of B-52B at Seattle.
       *JUNE 29:* First B-52 delivered to SAC's 93rd Bomb Wing, Castle Air Force Base, California.
       *DECEMBER 7:* First Wichita-built B-52 rolled out.

1956   *MARCH 9:* First flight of B-52C at Seattle.
       *MAY 14:* First flight of B-52D at Wichita.
       *JUNE 14:* Delivery of first B-52D to Castle Air Force Base from Wichita.
       *AUGUST 27:* Preliminary authorization received from the Air Force for B-52G production.
       *SEPTEMBER 28:* First flight of B-52D at Seattle.
       *NOVEMBER 25:* Eight B-52s complete record nonstop flights (Operation Quick Kick) of up to 17,000 miles, taking them over the North Pole—one in the air for 31½ hours.
       *DECEMBER 6:* Announcement made that B-52 to be awarded Collier Trophy for 1956.

1957   *JANUARY 18:* Three B-52s land at March Air Force Base, California, after flying around the world in 45 hours and 19 minutes. Averaging 530 MPH during the 24,325-mile flight from Castle Air Force Base, California, they more than cut in half the previous record set by a Boeing B-50 in 1949.
       *OCTOBER 3:* First flight of B-52E at Seattle.
       *OCTOBER 17:* First flight of B-52E at Wichita.
       *NOVEMBER 17:* Six B-52s land at Plattsburgh Air Force Base, New York, after flying nonstop round trip between the United States and Buenos Aires, Argentina, in 21 hours and 42 minutes. Total distance was 10,425 miles.

1958   *MAY 6:* First flight of B-52F at Seattle.
       *MAY 14:* First flight of B-52F at Wichita.
       *JULY 23:* First B-52G rolled out at Wichita.
       *OCTOBER 27:* First B-52G flight.
       *NOVEMBER 1:* First B-52G delivered to Air Research and Development Command.
       *DECEMBER 15:* Record nonstop, 18-hour, unrefueled flight of more than 9,000 miles completed by a B-52G manned by a Boeing Wichita crew.

1959   *FEBRUARY 13:* First B-52G delivered to SAC, Travis Air Force Base, California.
       *FEBRUARY 25:* Last Seattle-built B-52 (an "F" model) delivered to the Air Force.
       *AUGUST 1:* An Air Force manned B-52G landed at Edwards Air Force Base, California, to complete a 28-hour, nonstop flight of 12,942 miles. The flight took the bomber over all state capitals in the continental United States, including Alaska and the District of Columbia.
       *SEPTEMBER 4:* Announcement that The Boeing Company, Wichita, received a production go-ahead on the B-52H.

1960   *MARCH 2:* A SAC crew from Eglin Air Force Base, Florida, becomes the first Air Force crew to launch both Hound Dog missiles on a single flight over the Atlantic missile range.
       *APRIL 12:* A B-52G armed with two Hound Dog missiles took off from Eglin Air Force Base, Florida, flew to the North Pole and returned to the Atlantic missile range to score a successful Hound Dog launch. The 22-hour flight covered 10,800 miles nonstop.
       *SEPTEMBER 23:* Last B-52G rolled out from Boeing Wichita final assembly.
       *SEPTEMBER 30:* First B-52H rolled out from the production line in Wichita.
       *DECEMBER 14:* SAC B-52G flew 10,000-mile closed-circuit course (from Edwards Air Force Base and return) nonstop and without refueling.

1961   *MARCH 16:* First B-52H flight at Wichita.
       *MAY 9:* First B-52H delivered to SAC at Wurtsmith Air Force Base, Michigan.

1962   *JANUARY 11:* Minot Air Force Base operational B-52H flew 12,519 nonstop miles from Kadena Air Base, Okinawa, to Torrejon Air Base, Madrid, Spain, in 21 hours and 52 minutes to set or break eleven distance, course, and speed records without refueling.

  *JUNE 6-7:* SAC B-52H flew 11,303 miles unrefueled from Seymour-Johnson Air Force Base, North Carolina, over North America and return.

  *JUNE 22:* Last B-52H rolled from final assembly, halting B-52 production program that dated back to November 1951, when first model left Boeing Seattle (467 B-52s built at Wichita).

  *OCTOBER 26:* Last B-52H delivered to SAC at Minot Air Force Base, North Dakota.

1963   *NOVEMBER 1:* B-52H flown by Boeing Wichita crew completed 26-hour and 26-minute continuous test flight, covering 12,400 statute miles. Aircraft flew over all U.S. border states collecting dynamic loads data.

**Boeing B-52 Specifications**

Takeoff Weight: >450,000 lbs. (A-F)

>488,000 lbs. (G, H)

Speed: 650 MPH

Engines: 8

Thrust per Engine: >10,000 lbs. (A-G)
>17,000 lbs. (H)

Unrefueled Range: > 6,000 miles (A-F)
> 7,500 miles (G)
>10,000 miles (H)

Altitude: >50,000 ft.

Armament: 4 50-cal. machine guns (A-G)
1 20-mm Gatling Cannon (H)

Bomb Load: >20,000 lbs.

Crew: 6

DIMENSIONS

Wingspan: 185 ft.
Sweepback: 35°
Length: 156 ft. (A-F)
160 ft. (G)
Tail Height: 48 ft. (A-F)
40 ft. 8 in. (G, H)

| YEAR | PRODUCTION SITE | | TOTAL |
|---|---|---|---|
| | Wichita | Seattle | |
| 1954 | 0 | 5 | 5 |
| 1955 | 0 | 34 | 34 |
| 1956 | 10 | 65 | 75 |
| 1957 | 78 | 96 | 174 |
| 1958 | 91 | 65 | 156 |
| 1959 | 108 | 10 | 118 |
| 1960 | 73 | 0 | 73 |
| 1961 | 62 | 0 | 62 |
| 1962 | 45 | 0 | 45 |
| Totals | 467 | 275 | 742 |
| **MODEL** | | | |
| B-52A | - - | 3 | 3 |
| B-52B | - - | 50 | 50 |
| B-52C | - - | 35 | 35 |
| B-52D | 69 | 101 | 170 |
| B-52E | 58 | 42 | 100 |
| B-52F | 45 | 44 | 89 |
| B-52G | 193 | - - | 193 |
| B-52H | 102 | - - | 102 |
| Totals | 467 | 275 | 742 |

**B-52 Deliveries
(by Year, Model, Production Site)**

*During the testing of the B-52, Boeing conducted strenuous wing testing. This illustration shows how far the pulling and pressing went. (courtesy Boeing)*

*The first Stratofortress, the B-52A, Serial Number 2001. The A models never entered SAC service. (courtesy Boeing)*

*It was a proud moment for Boeing when the beautiful new A model rolled out. (courtesy Boeing)*

*An early B Model in flight (above). Note the shiny new aluminum of the machine. Also note the small "US Air Force"
which would be increased greatly in size in the later models, such as the C model at right. (courtesy U.S. Air Force)*

The first Wichita-built B-52D is shown during a test flight prior to its delivery to the U.S. Air Force. The 650-MPH bomber made its maiden flight on May 14, 1956. On June 26, a SAC crew flew it to Castle AFB, California, where it joined the 93rd Bomb Wing. (courtesy Boeing)

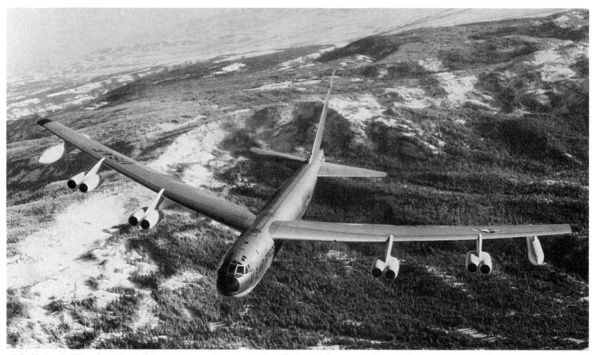

Of all the B-52s, the D model was the version produced in the largest numbers. Of the 170 built, 101 were constructed in Seattle, the others in Wichita. (courtesy Boeing)

*This D model, a Vietnam veteran, was installed as a monument at the U.S. Air Force Academy. (courtesy U.S. Air Force)*

*Later versions of the B-52D were characterized by tall black tails.*

21

*The D model shown here would carry much of the brunt of the Vietnam bombing load and would be heavily modified late in its career. (courtesy U.S. Air Force)*

*Exactly 100 of the D model were built. The Boeing-Wichita facility assumed the production lead by building 58 of the 100. (courtesy Boeing)*

*This is the first production E model, shown making a low-level test flight. (courtesy Boeing)*

*Many improvements were incorporated into the B-52G. The model was easily recognizable by the shortened vertical fin, which would be carried into the final H model. (courtesy Boeing)*

*A brand new B-52G skates over a cloud layer. The 193 B-52Gs were all produced at the Wichita production facility. (courtesy Boeing)*

*With its left external pylon racks empty and one ALCM missing from the right rack, this G bird roars across a clear sky. (courtesy U.S. Air Force)*

*Externally, the B-52H closely resembled the G model, except for the two-step appearance of the then-new turbofan engines. (courtesy U.S. Air Force)*

*A 1981 shot of a B-52H landing with a rear drag shute deployed during Exercise Busy Prairie II at Biggs Army Airfield, Texas. (courtesy U.S. Air Force)*

*With wings attached, these late-model B-52s were nearing production completion. (courtesy Boeing)*

# 3

# Improvements

THE B-52 WOULD HAVE TO RATE AS THE MOST HIGHLY-MODIFIED AIR-craft in Air Force history. As the plane has aged, the structure has been strengthened and the avionics and electronics improved so much that the planes are a far cry from what they were when they rolled off the production line. Many of the modifications and changes were also required because of the mission changes of the plane over the years. The B-52 evolved from the original mission of a high-altitude strategic bomber to an iron-bomb hauler during the Vietnam era—to an air-to-surface missile carrier in the 1980s. Still other B-52s found important roles as research-and-development and carrier aircraft in the development of missile and space vehicles.

The 1960s saw the first of the B-52's many modifications, the so-called Mod 1000 changes, which enabled the plane to perform high-speed low-level penetration flights while still maintaining its high-altitude capability. Other modifications made during that time period included the addition of various missile-carrying capabilities and electronic countermeasure systems to counter increased sophistication of enemy air defense systems.

Providing the Stratofortress with adequate structural integrity became a serious problem in the 1960s, as the earlier versions approached the end of their structural lifetimes. Engineering changes were made to guard against further deterioration and structural fatigue.

In 1963, plans were developed to expand the conventional capabilities of the heavy bomber. Five years later, at the peak of the Vietnam conflict, the modified D models could deliver four times the conventional bomb load of the unmodified versions: up to 84 bombs of the 500-pound class, or 24 750-pounders. An additional 24 750-pounders could be carried on external racks under the wings. B-52s so equipped were able to carry a total bomb load of about

60,000 pounds—an increase of 31,750 pounds over the normal payload. Another benefit derived from the modification was the ability to convert the aircraft's bomb-carrying equipment from nuclear to non-nuclear configurations and back.

Another effective modification effort was the B-52 quick-start package. Cartridge/pneumatic starters, installed on all eight engines on G and H models, allowed the simultaneous starting of all engines. By the mid-1970s this change had been made to the entire B-52G/H fleet.

By 1976 the same fleet had been retrofitted with the Electro-Optical Viewing System (EVS). The EVS provides the crew with an improved flight hazard avoidance capability, enabling the airplane to fly low-level in a "closed curtain" environment. It also allows the crew to assess strike target damage and avoid low-level terrain features. The EVS consists of two steerable sensors, one a low-light-level TV camera and the other an infrared unit. Mounted in turrets under the nose, and looking forward and downward, they transmit a picture of the terrain in TV display form to the cockpit and navigator stations.

The B-52 models have seen several different paint schemes. The initial Stratoforts rolled out in bare metal until the mid-1950s, when a special thermal-reflective paint was applied to the aircraft's exposed underside. Then, starting in 1965, SAC Stratoforts went into the paint shops to receive a camouflage job: green-and-tan upper and white underside. It wasn't long, however, before a shiny black finish was applied to the white underbelly and vertical fin.

In the late 1970s, another extensive electronic improvement was made to the G/H fleet—the Offensive Avionics System (OAS). The goal of the OAS program was to improve the bombers' navigational and delivery systems, reduce support costs, and most importantly, to provide an air-launched cruise missile capability. Major components of the system included a new computer for navigation and weapons delivery, an altitude heading reference system, a radar altimeter, an extremely accurate inertial navigation system (INS), and common strategic Doppler radar for the INS.

Even the older D models (all of which have since been deactivated) underwent changes through the mid-1970s. The old birds were modified to carry weapons for conventional bombing, anti-tank warfare, and even anti-ship operations. Major structural changes, completed in 1977 at a cost of $200 million, consisted of replacing wing panels, fuselage skirts, and wiring in the wings.

Improvements continued on the last two models into the 1980s with the installation of an improved Strategic Radar Program (SRP). With terrain-avoidance and ground-mapping capabilities, the system replaced some 50 separate radar boxes with just eight new ones.

Other smaller improvements (too numerous to mention them all) continue to be made, including an environmental control system, fuel quantity indicating system, defensive system updates, electromagnetic hardening (EMP), and the common strategic rotary launcher, which enables the B-52 to carry a wide variety of weapon systems. With an operational capability projected for the late 1980s, the Integrated Conventional Stores Management System (ICSMS) will enable the B-52G to send instructions to "smart" weapons concerning the route of travel, destination, and priority of targets. And there are more improvements being planned for the 1990s.

Some one-of-a-kind B-52s have served as a flying test beds. Probably the best known B-52 applications were as "mother ship" carriers for some of the famous X planes, including the manned, rocket-powered X-15. The so-called NB-52 aircraft was also used to carry the X-24 family of hypersonic research vehicles.

During 1973 an NB-52 equipped with a series of forward canards participated in a program to investigate future superstable aircraft. The Control Configured Vehicle (CCV) program demonstrated that the speed of future aircraft need not be limited to avoid flutter or structural bending. The CCV modifications enabled the NB-52E to surpass its design flutter speed several times.

Two other B-52s served as test beds for large new jet engines. The TF-39 (engine for the Lockheed C-5A) and the JT9D (engine for the Boeing 747) were both flight tested on modified Stratofortresses. In each case the huge new engines were mounted on the right inboard engine pylon.

B-52s are turning up in the strangest places. A salvaged late-model B-52 fuselage was used for antenna pattern measurements at the Rome Air Development Center. In 1974, a surplus B-52D served as a test bed for a Boeing structural test. The test airplane, with its nose and tail removed, was inverted and placed in a support structure. Then test instrumentation was added, and the wing was loaded with lead shot and sandbags until the wing failed—providing data on the strength of fleet B-52s.

*A relatively recent appendage to the B-52 mother ship was the parachute unit for the space shuttle solid rocket boosters. (courtesy U.S. Air Force)*

*A B-52E equipped to perform testing of the new Boeing 747 engine. (courtesy Pratt and Whitney)*

*The General Electric powerplant for the Lockheed C-5A was also tested on a B-52 inboard pylon. (courtesy General Electric)*

*Often, portions of B-52s in the Davis-Monthan Air Force Base boneyard were brought back to life. This forward section of an early model was shipped by truck to Kelly Air Force Base to be modified for test purposes. (courtesy U.S. Air Force)*

*At left, the "eyelids" of the Electro-Optical Viewing System (white turrets below the aircraft's nose) on this B-52H are in the protective closed position. Below, the sensors are exposed. (courtesy U.S. Air Force)*

*Many B-52 modifications were accomplished at this massive facility at Kelly Air Force Base. (courtesy U.S. Air Force)*

*An excess B-52D aircraft was used in a special wing-loading test at the Boeing-Wichita plant. The test was performed after the engines and a major portion of the fuselage were removed. (courtesy Boeing)*

*Under the so-called Pacer Plank program, 80 B-52Ds were extensively modified at the Wichita plant. The program was accomplished in the late 1970s with the modification allowing the aircraft to carry internally an increased number of conventional high-explosive bombs. (courtesy Boeing)*

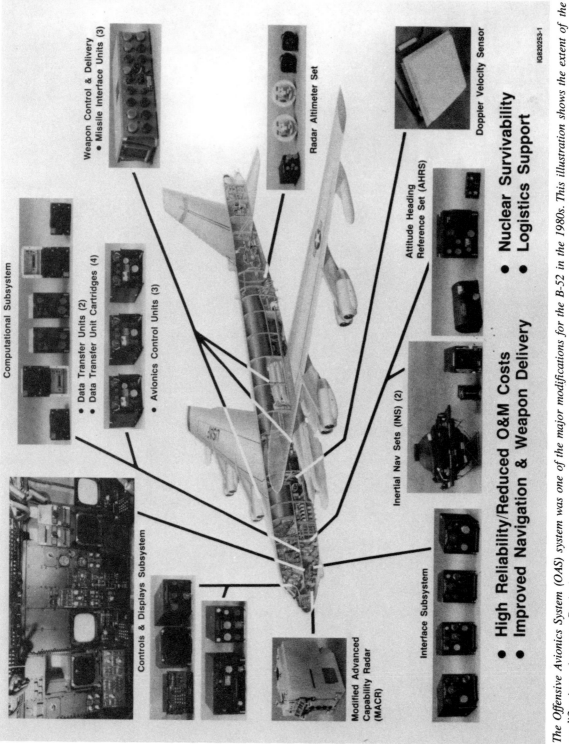

Weapon Control & Delivery
• Missile Interface Units (3)

Radar Altimeter Set

Doppler Velocity Sensor

Computational Subsystem

• Data Transfer Units (2)
• Data Transfer Unit Cartridges (4)

• Avionics Control Units (3)

Attitude Heading
Reference Set (AHRS)

Inertial Nav Sets (INS) (2)

Controls & Displays Subsystem

Modified Advanced
Capability Radar
(MACR)

Interface Subsystem

IG820253-1

• **High Reliability/Reduced O&M Costs**    • **Nuclear Survivability**
• **Improved Navigation & Weapon Delivery**  • **Logistics Support**

*The Offensive Avionics System (OAS) system was one of the major modifications for the B-52 in the 1980s. This illustration shows the extent of the modifications. (courtesy Boeing)*

*This vintage B-52 at Davis-Monthan AFB contributed one of its engines to a brother in Vietnam. (courtesy U.S. Air Force)*

*Modifications have been made continuously for many years. Here are some of the many changes made on the G model. (courtesy Boeing)*

*Parked in a "woven" pattern, these old B-52s await their fate at Davis-Monthan Air Force Base. (courtesy U.S. Air Force)*

# 4
# Weapons

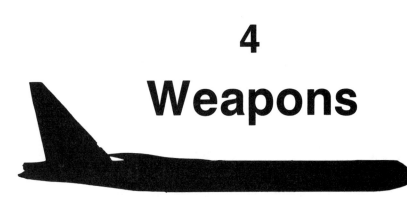

VERSATILITY AND FLEXIBILITY ARE ONLY TWO OF THE SUPER-
latives applicable to the B-52. Designed to perform a high-altitude
nuclear deterrence function, the Stratofort has performed a multitude
of undesigned-for functions, including carrying ballistic and cruise
standoff missiles, air-breathing decoy missiles, and conventional iron
bombs. And there could be additional new weapons before the last
Stratofort is retired.

The B-52 standoff role was best typified by the pairs of AGM-28B
jet-powered Hound Dog missiles the Stratofort carried starting in
1960. The Hound Dogs were carried on wing-mounted pylons between the fuselage and inboard engines. The missiles extended the
operations reach of the B-52 by more than 500 miles and permitted
one bomber to knock out several targets hundreds of miles apart.
The Hound Dog's inertial navigation system was pre-set for a mission
but could be retargeted prior to its release from the aircraft. The
42-foot-long missile could fly at 50,000-foot altitudes at a speed of
1,200 MPH. A unique B-52/Hound Dog interplay occurred because
the Hound Dog's 7,500-pound-thrust engines could be used to
augment the B-52 thrust in flight. The Hound Dog's tanks were then
refilled in flight from the B-52 tanks.

Today, more than 130 B-52s are modified to carry AGM-86B
air-launched cruise missiles (ALCMs). As many as 20 of these
subsonic, terrain-following missiles can be carried on a B-52. In
keeping with the SALT II agreement, the first B-52Gs modified to
carry ALCMs were delivered with 125-inch long strakelets—
aerodynamic fairings attached to the wings to make the aircraft
distinguishable from other B-52s not armed with cruise missiles.

The approximate 1500-mile range of the AGM-86B exceeds the performance of the earlier cruise missile, the Hound Dog, by over one

thousand miles. All twenty ALCMs are controlled by the triple-redundant Offensive Avionics System computer, enabling the navigator and radar navigator to program missile guidance to independent targets while airborne. The first ALCM weapon system became operational at Griffiss Air Force Base, New York, in December 1982. In 1986, the 131st B-52 was equipped with the ALCM system, exceeding the SALT II limits.

In February 1960, the Air Force had approved development of a long-range ballistic missile that could be launched against ground targets from high-flying jet bombers, a weapon more sophisticated with greater accuracy and range (1,150 miles) than any previous air-to-surface missile. The missile was called the Skybolt (GAM-87A) and the carrying bombers were to be the B-52H and RAF Vulcan jet bombers. Each Stratofort was to carry four Skybolts, two under each wing on inverted-T pylons. But the program was soon to be cancelled and the B-52Hs were adapted to carry the Hound Dog.

Some 281 B-52G and B-52H models were modified to carry the next weapon system, the Short Range Attack Missile (AGM-69A SRAM). Providing a new dimension to the B-52's offensive strike capability, the SRAM is a 14-foot-long missile weighing only 2,230 pounds. Inertially guided, the missile is powered by a two-pulse, solid-propellant rocket motor, carries a nuclear warhead, and can be retargeted aboard the aircraft prior to launch. The B-52, FB-111, and B-1B bomber all can carry the SRAM. The B-52 can carry up to 20 SRAMs on wing pylons and a rotary launcher, firing either singly or in salvo, and demonstrating a variety of trajectories from different directions. Sixteen B-52 and two FB-111 units were equipped with the SRAM.

As the B-52s aged through the 1960s and into the 1970s, significant electronic improvements were made to the Stratoforts. One countermeasure was the small diversionary missile, Quail. This jet-powered decoy was to be dropped from the Stratofort's bomb bays; the Quail's electronics would then simulate a B-52 for enemy radar scopes. Chaff-dispensing pods were also carried by some B-52's. These pods were located on a wing pylon between the engine pods. 2.75-inch rockets pushed the chaff outward in front of the aircraft for radar deception.

SCAD was the acronym for Subsonic Cruise Armed Decoy, which was to be the replacement for the Quail, but with one added dimension. In addition to its decoy mission, the SCAD was to carry a warhead. The SCAD was to have been launched from the SRAM launcher, but the program, initiated in June 1972, was cancelled in early 1974. Later that year, an air-launched cruise missile with a diversional mission was considered to replace the cancelled SCAD, but that program never materialized either. ◢██◣

*A sign of the 1960s. An unpainted B-52G carrying two Hound Dog missiles. The AGM-28B Hound Dog was first introduced to the B-52 fleet in 1960. The G and H model 52s carried the missile, one under each wing. (courtesy U.S. Air Force)*

*Once the Hound Dogs had served their purpose, they were retired to final storage at Davis-Monthan Air Force Base, Arizona. (courtesy U.S. Air Force)*

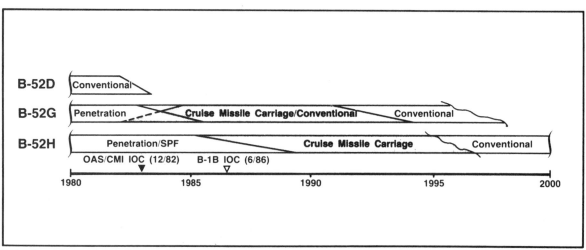

| | | | | | |
|---|---|---|---|---|---|
| **B-52D** | Conventional | | | | |
| **B-52G** | Penetration | Cruise Missile Carriage/Conventional | | Conventional | |
| **B-52H** | Penetration/SPF | | Cruise Missile Carriage | Conventional | |

OAS/CMI IOC (12/82) ▼    B-1B IOC (6/86) ▽

1980          1985          1990          1995          2000

*This chart shows the evolution of weapon use aboard the last three versions of the B-52. (courtesy Boeing)*

*One air-launched cruise missile (ALCM) awaits the arrival of others, all to be loaded onto the wings of a Stratofortress. (courtesy U.S. Air Force)*

44

*An outboard load of ALCMs prior to installation on a B-52H. (courtesy Boeing)*

*Mounting the ALCMs on the underwing pylon requires the use of specialized ground support equipment and a crew of trained Air Force technicians. (courtesy U.S. Air Force)*

*A B-52G with its complement of 12 pylon-mounted AGM-86B ALCMs stands ready on the Griffiss Air Force Base flight line. (courtesy Boeing)*

*An ALCM over a western test range, verifying its precision navigation capability. (courtesy Boeing)*

*This B-52G carried the strakelets (not visible in this photo) that identified it as a cruise missile hauler. (courtesy U.S. Air Force)*

*The rotary launcher can hold ALCMs . . .*

48

*. . . or the earlier SRAMs. (courtesy U.S. Air Force)*

*SRAM loading by SAC munitions specialists readying a B-52 for alert. (courtesy U.S. Air Force)*

*Internal bomb bay carriage is illustrated by this AGM-86B on the Common Rotary Launcher. (Courtesy U.S. Air Force)*

*A load of iron bombs can also be tucked away in the bomb bay. (courtesy U.S. Air Force)*

*A rather new weapon for the B-52 is the Harpoon ATM-84A missile system. A load of the missiles is shown here on the pylon of a B-52G. (courtesy Boeing)*

The deadly tail stinger of the
B-52H. (courtesy U.S. Air Force)

Earlier models carried the four-gun version
shown here. (courtesy U.S. Air Force)

*A G model carries a full load of SRAMs. B-52Gs and Hs were configured at one time to carry up to 20 SRAMs. The Stratofort/SRAM combination provided an elusive target capable of either high or low altitude launch at stand-off ranges or from deep within enemy territory. (courtesy Boeing)*

*A contrail drifts across the sky behind the vertical tail of this B-52H when it was a part of the 17th Bombardment Wing at Wright-Patterson Air Force Base during the 1970s. (courtesy Dale Witt)*

PLATE 1. The roll-out of the XB-52 one rainy night in Seattle was shrouded in secrecy as evidenced by the large tarp that completely covered the airplane. (Courtesy Boeing)

PLATE 2. A B-52G carrying a full external load of SRAM missiles. (Courtesy Boeing)

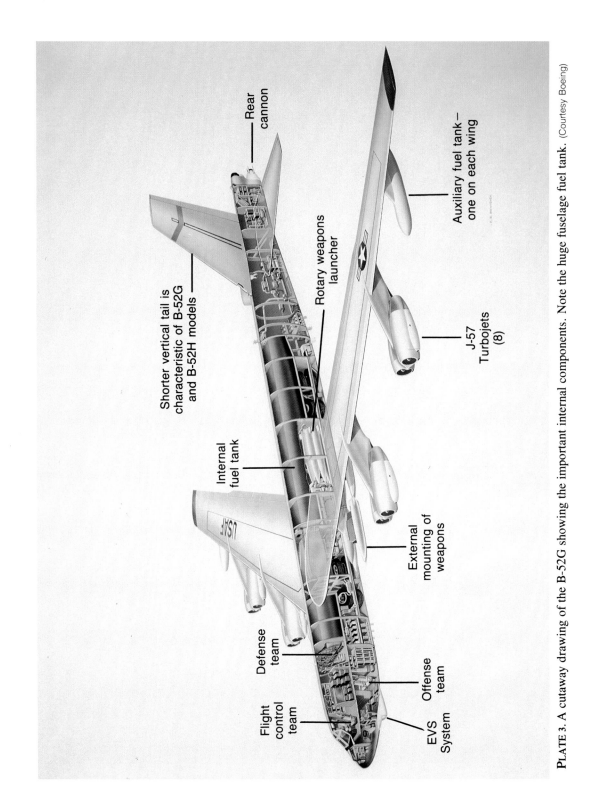

Rear cannon

Auxiliary fuel tank— one on each wing

Shorter vertical tail is characteristic of B-52G and B-52H models

Rotary weapons launcher

J-57 Turbojets (8)

Internal fuel tank

External mounting of weapons

Defense team

Offense team

Flight control team

EVS System

PLATE 3. A cutaway drawing of the B-52G showing the important internal components. Note the huge fuselage fuel tank. (Courtesy Boeing)

**PLATE 4.** A **B-52G** majestically flies over the western United States. There is a chance that this version could be retired by the early 1990s.
(Courtesy U.S. Air Force)

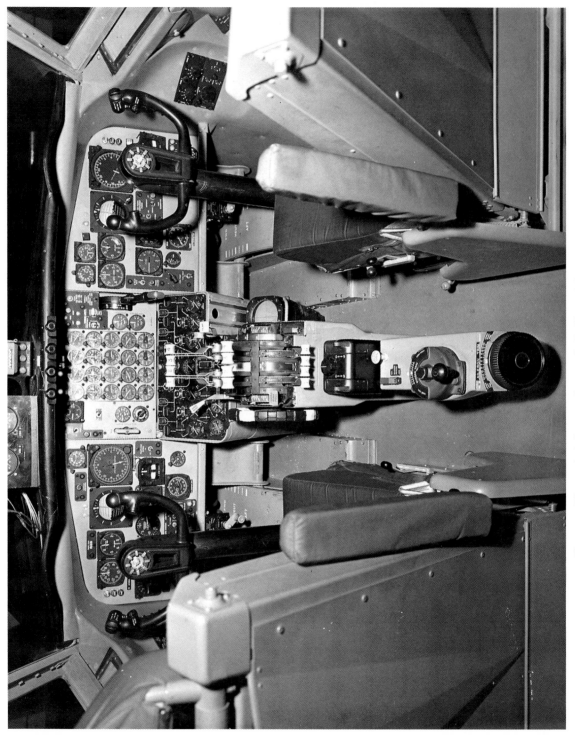

PLATE 5. The cockpit layout of an early B-52 model. (Courtesy Boeing)

**PLATE 6.** There's a sweeping beauty to the pylon-mounted engine pods on this B-52H. (Courtesy Dale Witt)

**PLATE 7.** A flight of three B-52s drops 1,000- and 750-pound bombs on a target 25 miles from Bien Hoa Air Base in Vietnam. (Courtesy U.S. Air Force)

PLATE 8. A B-52 sits on alert at a SAC base. (Courtesy Boeing)

PLATE 9. A 1980s alert has this B-52 crew dashing on a wet tarmac. (Courtesy U.S. Air Force)

PLATE 10. A KC-10 gives a B-52H all it can handle during a refueling operation. (Courtesy U.S. Air Force)

PLATE 11. In the 1980s, the G models got a new camouflage paint job. (Courtesy U.S. Air Force)

**PLATE 12.** This B-52G was assigned to Fairchild Air Force Base, Washington in the late 1970s. The G and H models can be distinguished from the earlier models by the shorter vertical stabilizer. (Courtesy U.S. Air Force)

**PLATE 13.** It eventually happens to all Air Force aircraft. Here at Davis-Monthan Air Force Base is a field of early model B-52s that are slowly being cannibalized (note the missing pieces). (Courtesy U.S. Air Force)

# 5

# Operations

THE STRATEGIC AIR COMMAND WAS FORMED ON MARCH 21, 1946 TO perpetuate the strategic bombing superiority that had helped bring Allied victory during World War II. General George C. Kenny was appointed commander and given the mandate of building an organization capable of conducting long-range offensive operations in any part of the world. He began with a total of 37,000 military men and 950 aircraft—about 300 of which were vintage B-17s, B-25s, and B-29s. Four months after he started, the atomic bomb test at Bikini displayed the Command's nuclear capability and ushered in an era of rapid expansion and buildup.

In 1948, two aircraft were delivered, the B-36 and B-50, and General Curtis E. LeMay took command. The headquarters moved from Andrews AFB, Maryland, to Offutt AFB, Nebraska, and in-flight refueling was introduced, giving SAC's bombers true "intercontinental" range.

During the Korean War, SAC B-29s made history in their first real test of combat readiness, dropping 167,000 tons of conventional bombs and destroying every strategic industrial target in North Korea in three months. In August 1953 the explosion of the first Soviet hydrogen bomb emphasized the Red nuclear threat, and all phases of SAC training were pushed ahead at full speed.

New aircraft were swiftly introduced to replace obsolete systems. By the mid-1950s, the first all-jet B-47 bomber had replaced the B-29s and B-50s, and the KC-97 was the main refueling tanker. In 1955 the B-52 made its appearance on the SAC scene. By the end of the 1950s, a portion of the B-52 bomber force was on 15-minute ground alert, and airborne alert and dispersal concepts were being tested to offset decreasing warning times caused by the growing Soviet strategic missile forces.

For a period of time, a certain percentage of the B-52 force was constantly airborne, but this practice proved impractical for a number of reasons (especially fuel consumption and wear-and-tear), and a ground alert system with super-quick response times was developed. The ground alert technique continues to be employed today with response times measured in minutes and seconds from Klaxon sounding to ''wheels in the well.''

The B-52's first chance to respond during an imminent war situation came in 1962 during the Cuban missile crisis. During this tense time SAC began dispersing aircraft, moving some of its Florida-based B-52 bombers and KC-135 tankers to other U.S. bases to make room for the tactical aircraft buildup there.

On October 25, 1962, SAC's help was required in locating Soviet surface shipping, and SAC B-47 reconnaissance aircraft and KC-97 tankers began combing an 825,000-square-mile rectangle north of Cuba between Bermuda and the Azores. On these missions hundreds of visual and radar sightings were made, from high altitudes to as low as 300 feet. Initial contact with the Soviet ships, however, had been made within hours by B-52 aircraft flying alert missions.

B-52s took to the air on 24-hour missions designed to (1) keep them within reach of potential targets at all times and (2) guarantee the survival of a large part of SAC's strike aircraft from any attack, including one without warning. From its beginning on October 22 to its end on November 21 (when routine alert training was resumed), SAC bombers and tankers flew more than 2,000 sorties, calling for nearly 50,000 hours of continuous flight. Under constant positive control, airborne alert aircraft flew more than 20 million miles and transferred some 70 million gallons of fuel during more than 4,000 aerial refuelings.

Almost three years later, the Stratofort was called on again. This time it was for real. From June 18, 1965 to January 27, 1973, B-52s flew conventional bombing missions almost daily against communist forces in Vietnam. Crews on temporary duty from their home bases in the United States and operating from U-Tapao, Thailand, and Anderson AFB, Guam, flew B-52s (each carrying up to 60,000 pounds of bombs) for strategic bombing, close air support, and interdiction missions. B-52 strikes continued against military targets in Laos until April 17, 1973, and in support of friendly forces in Cambodia until August 15, 1973.

During their wide-ranging operations in South Vietnam, the B-52s were used to deliver huge tonnages of bombs in precision high-altitude strikes against hidden enemy concentrations. Usually flying in three-plane cells, the B-52s helped clear paths for tactical ground operations targets that were usually well-hidden. Targets included supply zones, area headquarters, and troop concentrations.

With the late 1960s' buildup of U.S. forces in Southeast Asia, the Stratoforts increased their raids in support of ground operations. Raids concentrated on such areas as the Demilitarized Zone, where the enemy was attempting to move supplies to the south.

B-52s played an important part in the now-famous Khe Sanh operation. Early in 1968, 6,000 Marines and South Vietnamese Rangers were surrounded at this austere outpost by 20,000 North Vietnamese troops. While tactical fighters harassed the enemy, the B-52s dropped up to 1,400 tons of ordnance daily with devastating results. The effectiveness of the B-52 response was intensified by the arrival of a three-plane cell every 90 minutes round-the-clock. During the Khe Sanh operations, the Stratoforts rose for some 2,600 sorties, delivering over 75,000 tons of ordnance.

The nuclear bomber had demonstrated with conventional ordnance the effectiveness of World War II saturation bombing. But the biggest operation for the B-52s would come in December 1972. The mission would be "up north," and the challenge would be the toughest the old bird would probably every face. The targets would be installations and transshipment points near Hanoi and Haiphong in North Vietnam. It was hoped that the LINEBACKER II operation would bring an end to American involvement in Vietnam. A little-known fact is that this was not the first time the B-52s had ventured north. On April 17 of the same year, B-52s attacked targets near Haiphong with all aircraft returning safely.

B-52s had previously been under SAM attack in southern operations but these attacks had been few and scattered. During LINEBACKER II the B-52 would encounter its first massive SAM challenge, along with the menace of fighters. As it worked out, there were no Stratofort losses to MIGs, although some 32 came up to contest the B-52s.

The raids were carried out between December 18th and 29th—eleven fateful days. The Stratoforts (namely B-52Ds and B-52Gs) went in at night to prevent visual tracking, and proved to be just as effective at night. Flying LINEBACKER II during daylight hours wouldn't have afforded any advantage because the miserable weather would have afforded only 12 hours of visual bombing.

LINEBACKER II was a team effort—a highly coordinated, precisely run operation. Navy tactical aircraft and Marine fighters provided a protective combat screen and attacked targets near the coast. Air Force fighters provided protective escort for the B-52, combat air patrol, and defensive suppression for the Hanoi-Haiphong complex.

The B-52s also used chaff to confuse the enemy defenses.

Railroad targets were hit first, with 383 rail cars, 14 locomotives, 191 warehouses, and 2 bridges destroyed. Of the nine major storage areas in the general bombing area, 25 major, 26 small, and 29 other buildings were destroyed. The bombing was accurate and decisive. During the operation, over 20,000 tons were dropped, mostly by the B-52s. Fifteen of the giant Stratoforts were lost (on about 700 sorties), 10 of which went down in North Vietnamese territory. This loss, about 2 percent, was not as high as the pre-mission estimate of 3 percent. Nine other planes were damaged (two heavily), but all of these made it back safely. Nevertheless, the cost had been high, but the B-52s got the job done.

After Vietnam, the general missions of the remaining G and H models (all D models have been phased out) have continued to exploit strengths of the aircraft rather than the weaknesses caused by age and maintenance difficulties. The Strategic Projection Force (SPF) concept, spawned in the late 1970s, draws on the enormous payload, long range, and rapid response possible of the B-52 fleet. To prove this new conventional warfare capability, an Operational Readiness Inspection in the 1980s hit one B-52H unit with a unique flight mission. One entire squadron of H-model aircraft, their crews, ground crew chiefs, and their personal equipment were scrambled without extensive preparation on a 15-hour, nonstop mission to Anderson AFB, Guam. From that forward deployment location, extensive sea surveillance and long-range conventional training missions were conducted. This was the first time an entire squadron of H models had ever been deployed outside the continental U.S. The advanced systems and long range of the G and H models have made the SPF a credible complement to any conventional mission or engagement worldwide.

*Incendiary cluster bombs are loaded into a B-52 in January 1967. The bombs would set fires to burn away the heavy growth hiding enemy installations in South Vietnam. (courtesy U.S. Air Force)*

*A B-52 awaits its next mission from U-Tapao Air Base in Thailand after deployment from Guam during Typhoon Olga in October 1972. (courtesy U.S. Air Force)*

*A group of five B-52Ds move down the flight line at Anderson Air Force Base for a Southeast Asia mission. G models await their time on the left side of the picture. The G birds are characterized by their shorter vertical stabilizers. (courtesy U.S. Air Force)*

*A parade of B-52Ds stretches down the sloping plain at Anderson. (courtesy U.S. Air Force)*

*This camouflaged B-52D releases its 60,000-pound bomb load on enemy targets in Vietnam. Each of the bombers could carry up to eighty-four 500-pound bombs or fourty-two 750-pound bombs internally, and twenty-four 750-pound bombs externally on racks under the wings. (courtesy U.S. Air Force)*

*The exciting SAC alerts of an earlier time. Note the lack of camouflage paint on the aircraft. (courtesy U.S. Air Force)*

*A B-52G is shown being refueled by a KC-135 tanker. (courtesy Boeing)*

*A B-52H carrying a load of AGM-86B cruise missiles snuggles up to a tanker for a load of JP-4. (courtesy U.S. Air Force)*

*Movie star Jimmy Stewart, a Reserve General in the Air Force, flew B-52 missions and is shown here exiting the aircraft. (courtesy U.S. Air Force)*

# 6
# From the Cockpit

JUST ABOUT EVERY PLANE EVER BUILT EVENTUALLY GOT A NICKNAME or two. For the B-52, it was the unlikely title of BUFF, an acronym for "Big Ugly Fat Fellow." Where the name came from isn't clear, but it probably originated during the mid-1960s in Southeast Asia.

Even in the era of the C-5A and 747 jumbo jets, the B-52 is still an impressive aircraft. In fact, the B-52 eventually gained the FAA designation "JUMBO" because its latest authorized in-flight gross weight exceeds 500,000 pounds. With its long swept wings and arching tail, the B-52 belies its 1940s heritage. But even though pilots saw fit to slip "Ugly" in its nickname, the old bird has a majestic and domineering beauty. Like the lines of a classic car, BUFF never seems to get out of date.

Walking around the aircraft, you can't help but be impressed with the protrusions and hang-ons. The eight engines, mounted in pairs, are carried in sharply forward-raked pods under the thin high-speed wing. The stepped-diameter turbofans of the final H model are quite distinguishable from the trim lines of the earlier engines.

The landing gear seem insignificant when compared to the massive weight they support. The small outriggers on the wingtips barely plant themselves when the wings of a G or H model are bulging with fuel. When the wings are dry, the outriggers hang helplessly, grasping for the ground they can't reach. The outriggers do, however, tend to keep the plane from tipping when it is moving. BUFF pilots like to refer to them as "training wheels."

The giant Fowler flaps are staggering when fully extended (their position for both takeoff and landing). Their function is closely tied to the unique landing gear arrangement. Because the gear are in tandem, the B-52 must land aft-gear first. The giant flaps provide the necessary lift. If the forward gear hit first, the Stratofort has a tendency to skip back into the air.

The B-52 is a strange combination of the very strong and very weak. Although built to carry massive bomb loads over intercontinental distances, the aircraft is only stressed for about two G's. A B-52 pilot aptly described the fuselage as a pencil. "It can be pushed and pulled as long as the forces are applied along the fuselage centerline. But put a side pressure on it, and it can easily be broken."

The maximum skin thickness of the B-52 is 0.40 inch. A testament, however, to the B-52's strength and stamina occurred during a mid 1960s test flight of a B-52G. A violent gust tore away the airplane's rudder and most of the vertical fin, but the craft was able to make a safe landing 700 miles later.

Crawling into the innards of this behemoth, you quickly realize how small the crew area is. The complete crew of six is limited to the forward 15 percent of the aircraft during their long and tiring missions. The remainder of the bird, the majority of which is the weapons-carrying section, is not pressurized.

The cockpit is a cozy arrangement with a myriad of panels and instruments surrounding the pilot and co-pilot. Located between the seats are the eight throttles. Ejection from the aircraft is upward for the four crewmembers on the upper deck, while the other two are shot out the bottom of the plane.

Takeoff is one of the strangest characteristics of this bird. The B-52 does not rotate. As the eight wheels of the main gear leave the ground, the aircraft fuselage remains practically level. It looks like it's going up on an elevator, making you wonder where the lift comes from.

The way the wing is joined to the fuselage, and the giant flaps, explain this apparently strange phenomenon. The design of the Fowler flaps gives the aircraft high lift during takeoffs and landings with zero fuselage angle. The plane can maintain level flight even in a slight nose-down attitude, because of the wings' high angle of incidence. The Stratofort is, indeed, a unique flying machine.

Rolling down the runway, the droopy-winged Stratofort seems to first test the air's lift, starting at the wingtips. Then the vast expanse of wing, some 4,000 square feet, starts to take the hint and the droop disappears. Slowly the fuselage fights the bonds of earth bringing the gear struts up to maximum deflection till the rubber leaves the concrete.

To get the non-turbofan-equipped A-G models off the ground, hundreds of gallons of water must be injected through the eight engines for added thrust. But with the B-52H, it's an entirely different situation. With each of its turbofans kicking out some 17,000 pounds of thrust, the H model has power to burn. In fact, even when fully loaded, the B-52H doesn't need to use maximum power settings for takeoff.

The B-52H takeoff is characterized by relatively constant acceleration throughout the range of takeoff weights; this is accomplished by adjusting the throttle settings. For a lightweight takeoff, the takeoff speed is about 127 knots, while a heavyweight load needs about 160 knots to clear the runway. With its great power reserve, the B-52H can easily handle an engine-out situation during takeoff. The pilot maneuvers the rudder and juggles the throttles to take care of the thrust imbalance. Pilots of early-model B-52s tell of the muscles required to operate the manual flight control system. But the B-52G/H models are extremely light on the stick and need no trim tabs.

In flight, the B-52 is an extremely stable aircraft, mainly due to its tremendous weight and inertia. Once 240 tons of Stratofort is pointed in one direction, it doesn't want to change. Pilots say that the big bird takes turbulence and weather very smoothly; however, the tremendous inertia of the B-52's heavier weight ranges reduces the plane's responsiveness to pilot inputs during refueling operations. The G and H models' gross weight can grow from about 200,000 pounds to 525,000 pounds after a fill-up—a gain in excess of 160 tons. On its internal fuel supply alone the B-52H can fly twenty hours.

Getting the Stratofortress stopped after touchdown was another problem that faced the Boeing engineers. The B-52's formidable braking system normally absorbs enough energy to stop, simultaneously, 470 automobiles traveling at 50 MPH. Under full braking conditions, the energy absorbed would halt over 1,000 cars. Like the earlier B-47, the B-52 uses a braking parachute deployed from the rear of the aircraft.

The B-52 is a very forgiving aircraft—certainly much more so than the B-47 or B-58. Its big wings, adequate power, and superstrong landing gear help cover mistakes. Additionally, all B-52s seem to act almost identically—an extremely important safety factor because, unlike the World War II days, each crew now draws whatever aircraft is ready (not the same one every time). But the B-52 is not a pilot's airplane. It was built to be "directed" by the navigator and radar operator to put ordnance on target. And it continues to display this amazing weapons delivery capability in a myriad of new roles. New electronics, weapons, and missions are proving the versatility of B-52 aircraft and crews—just proving the Combat Crew Training School motto, *"You've got to be tough to fly the heavies."*

*The B-52H cockpit configuration is considerably different from the earlier versions of the big plane. (courtesy Dale Witt)*

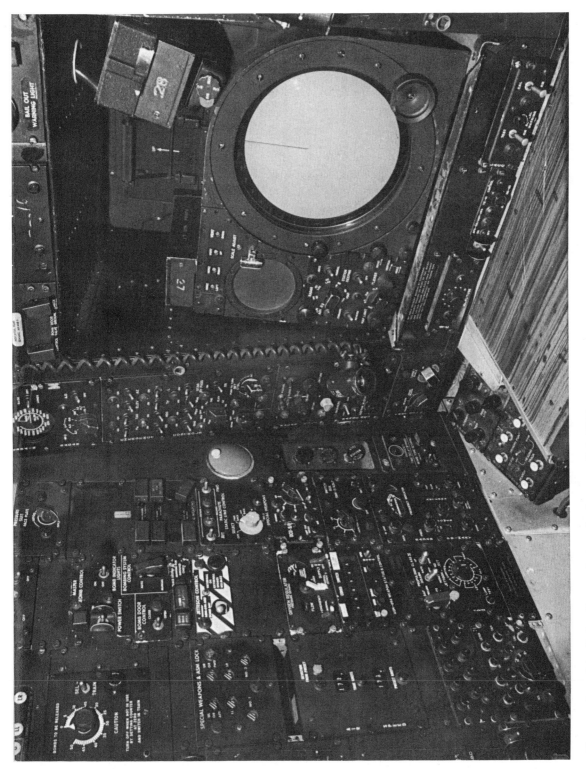

*Close-up view of the Radar Operator's console. (courtesy Dale Witt)*

*View of the consoles of the Radar Operator (left) and the Navigator (right). (courtesy Dale Witt)*

*A SAC maintenance man provides perspective on the size of the B-52H's turbofans. (courtesy Dale Witt)*

*The sealed engine pods of a B-52D Vietnam veteran on display at the Air Force Museum at Wright-Patterson Air Force Base.*

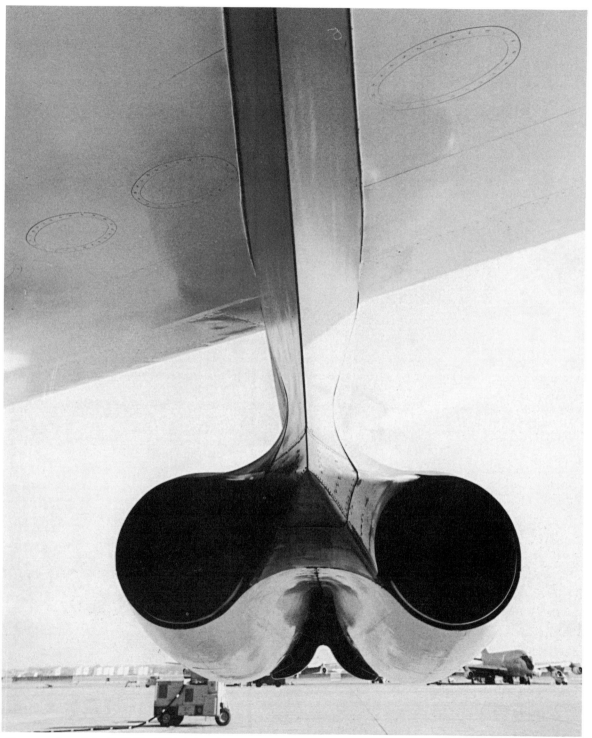

*The posterior of the B-52H's TF33-P-3 turbofans. (courtesy Dale Witt)*

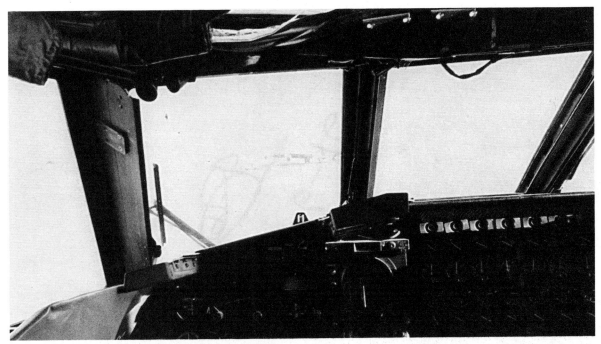

*The pilot's view from a B-52H. (courtesy Dale Witt)*

*This angle captures the classic lines and form of the Stratofortress. (courtesy Dale Witt)*

*The giant inboard Fowler flap in the fully extended position. (courtesy Dale Witt)*

The aft landing gear arrangement of the B-52D.

The B-52D forward landing gear.

The B-52H forward landing gear. Both sets of wheels must touch down simultaneously. Both sets can also be turned to permit a "crabbed" landing. (courtesy Dale Witt)

One of the most famous B-52 pictures ever taken. This B-52H, on a test flight, encountered severe turbulence and lost its rudder and most of its vertical fin, but was still able to make a safe landing. (courtesy U.S. Air Force)

*In 1969 a B-52 crew landed with four operative engines at Wurtsmith Air Force Base, Michigan, after Engines 5 and 6 burned and dropped off, and Engines 7 and 8 ran out of fuel. (courtesy U.S. Air Force)*

# 7
# The Future

THE B-52 COULD WELL BE THE LONGEST-SERVING U.S. MILITARY AIR-craft. Born in the 1950s, it will likely be used until the next century. With its many modifications and improvements over the years, the G and H models have remained viable weapon systems.

In the years to come, the B-52 will complement the new B-1B bomber and the Advanced Technology Bomber (ATB), which could come into the inventory in the 1990s. But even though the B-52 will probably be the first of the trio to be deactivated, its influence will continue to be felt. The offensive avionics for the B-1B were the offspring of the original B-52 OAS system. The rotary launcher, also developed for the B-52, is being tested in the B-1B and will be incorporated in the B-1B fleet as the B-52Hs retire.

The B-52 Stratofortress—a venerable old bird that just seems to go on forever!!

*For a number of years, different versions of the FB-111 were considered as replacements for the B-52. In the late 1980s, both aircraft are still operational with the Strategic Air Command. (courtesy U.S. Air Force)*

*The SRAM II missile system is a follow-on of the initial SRAM system carried on the B-52. This photo shows a test of the SRAM II's integral rocket ramjet propulsion system. As of this writing, this new missile will not be carried aboard the B-52 fleet. (courtesy U.S. Air Force)*

# OFFENSIVE & DEFENSIVE AVIONICS SYSTEMS

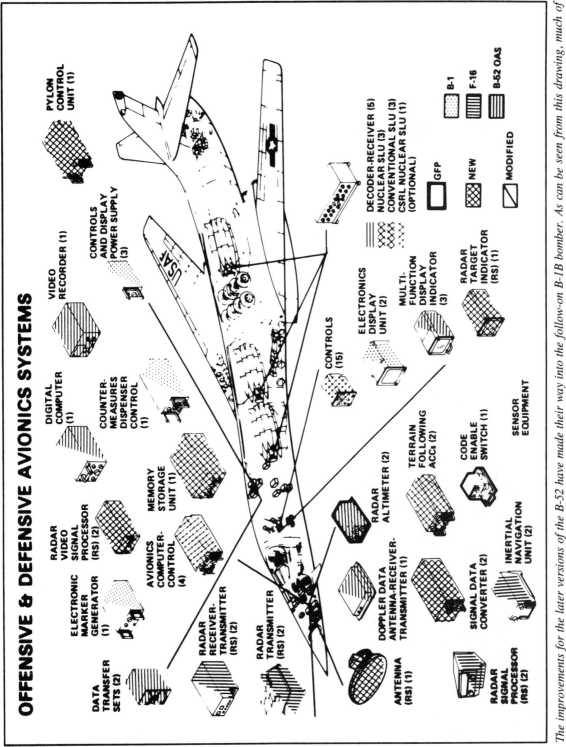

The improvements for the later versions of the B-52 have made their way into the follow-on B-1B bomber. As can be seen from this drawing, much of the B-52 OAS is now an important part of the B-1B. (courtesy Boeing)

*The B-1A was the first of the B-1s, but the program was cancelled in the late 1970s, again increasing the importance of the B-52 fleet. (courtesy U.S. Air Force)*

*Reactivated by President Reagan, the B-1B program will replace the B-52. One hundred of the B-1Bs were produced. (courtesy U.S. Air Force)*

# Index

Edited by Carl H. Silverman

# Other Bestsellers From TAB

☐ **U.S. CIVIL AIRCRAFT SERIES, VOL 9: ATC 801—ATC 817—Joseph P. Juptner**

This intriguing volume covers the last 17 Approved Type Certificated Aircraft plus a master index of the nine volume series, ATC update, group two section (Letter of Approval), limited type certificate (LTC), restricted category (AR), people of aviation index. Included are plane descriptions, histories, production and performance data, complete specifications, and other technical information. 240 pp., illustrated

**Hard    $19.95                              Book No. 29182**

☐ **"THERE I WAS . . . FLAT ON MY BACK"—Bob Stevens**

*"Stevens stands alone as a fine artist who has made sight gags out of any aerial peril survived . . . his work is perceptive, a fine technical caricature, very, very funny."*—**Los Angeles Times**

Here is the best of Bob's aviation cartooning—some of the best humor to come out of the last three air wars. Whether you are a pilot, navigator, bombardier, or "gravel agitator" you'll get a tremendous kick out of it all! 224 pp., Fully illustrated

**Paper    $11.95                              Book No. 28954**

☐ **IF YOU READ ME, ROCK THE TOWER—Bob Stevens**

A collection of aviation humor by internationally-known cartoonist Bob Stevens—creator of the popular comic "STOP SQUAWK!" in *Private Pilot*. Dedicated to all the airmen of World War II, Korea, and Vietnam, this is a compilation of cartoons, jokes, Air Force jargon, aircraft silhouettes, and barrack ballads—each one more hilarious than the last. And Bob Stevens draws his material from first-hand experience as a former Air Force Pilot and aviation enthusiast for over 42 years. 144 pp.

**Paper    $9.95                               Book No. 26505**

☐ **CHARIOTS FOR APOLLO: THE UNTOLD STORY BEHIND THE RACE TO THE MOON—Charles R. Pellegrino and Joshua Stoff**

Many books have been written about the astronauts who first set foot on the moon. But the hundreds and even thousands of designers, technicians, and others who made the lunar module possible have been little recognized. Here they are highlighted. You'll witness the political and scientific infighting that surrounded the project. You'll share the frustrations, the sacrifices, the uncertainties, and the humor that affected the ordinary people involved in the project. 256 pp., Two eight-page black & white photo sections

**Paper    $14.95                             Book No. 22923**

☐ **U.S. CIVIL AIRCRAFT SERIES: VOL. 7 ATC 601—ATC 700—Joseph P. Juptner**

A pictorially rich reference, Vol. 7 covers one hundred airplanes manufactured during the "Golden Age of Aviation" period (1936-1939). Included are such outstanding favorites as the Douglas DC-3, Benny Howard's "Damned Good Airplanes," the Taylorcraft, Piper's new "Cub" line, the brand-new "Aeronca" line, selection offered in "Waco" airplanes, the revolutionary Spartan "Executive," and the "Luscombe 8." 352 pp., 358 illus.

**Hard    $19.95                              Book No. 29174**

☐ **THE RED BARON—MANFRED VON RICHTHOFEN—Stanley M. Ulanoff (Col., USAR)**

Flying's greatest legend lives again in the personal diary and letters of the most famous air ace of World War I: Manfred Feiherr von Richthofen, the famed Red Baron. Included are his own accounts of many of his exploits and the story of his last battle in the words of the Canadian captain whose bullet killed him. Includes over 60 drawings of the planes and their weapons, top German aces of 1914-1918, and 40 historic photographs. 240 pp.

**Hard    $12.95                              Book No. 27925**

☐ **AERO AVIATION COLLEGE DIRECTORY—M. George Mandis**

The book lists 377 colleges and universities offering aviation courses, an aviation related degree, or extensive pilot training courses. It is a source reference for libraries, schools, colleges, counselors, educators, and individuals seeking information relative to aviation courses and careers. The book contains information regarding specific degree programs; flight training and ratings; flight training costs; certified flight instructor staff; and much more! 272 pp.

**Paper    $12.95                             Book No. 23029**

☐ **AUTOGIRO: THE STORY OF "THE WINDMILL PLANE"—George Townson**

If you're interested in the history of flying you won't want to miss this review of autorotation which led to the invention of the "windmill plane" . . . and later to the designing of the helicopter. Packed with photographs and drawings, this comprehensive pictorial portrays the development work of the Autogiro Company of America and its licenses from 1928 to 1943 with details on designs, construction and flight characteristics. 156 pp., illustrated

**Hard    $19.95                              Book No. 22900**

☐ **SPACE SHUTTLE LOG: THE FIRST 25 FLIGHTS—Gene Gurney and Jeff Forte**

The specifics of the space shuttle itself—how it functions what its purpose is, and why it is necessary are followed by an in-depth discussion of each of the 25 flights. The authors take great care to eliminate much of the technical jargon, and offer an honest, objective, historical record of the space shuttle program. This is your opportunity to explore the ins and outs of the U.S. Space Shuttle Program to date. 304 pp., 270 illus.

**Paper $18.95**        **Book No. 22390**

☐ **AERO SERIES VOL. 29: GENERAL DYNAMICS F-11 ''Aardvark''—Jay Miller**

General Dynamics awesome variable-sweep-wing F-111 is unquestionably the most controversial operational warplane of our time, politically sensitive, economically catastrophic, and mechanically overwhelming, it was in every respect the most complex and extraordinary flying machine of its day. This book provides a synopsis of its genesis, a study of its anatomy, and a review of its service career. 104 pp., illustrated, 4-page color section

**Paper $9.95**        **Book No. 20606**

☐ **VOL. 33, THE McDONNELL DOUGLAS APACHE—Frank Colucci**

The AH-64 Apache is the newest, most advanced attack helicopter ever built. It took 13 years and the best defense contractors in the business to make the machine. But the results were worth the wait. Tested performance capabilities dramatically exceeded specified requirements in target detection, acquisition, tracking, recognition and identification with direct view optics, television, and forward-looking infrared sensors. 112 pp., 104 illus., 8 pages in full color

**Paper $10.95**        **Book No. 20614**

☐ **STUDIES IN STARLIGHT: UNDERSTANDING OUR UNIVERSE—Charles J. Caes**

Man, for all his intelligence and technology, has yet to understand the power of radiant energies . . . or perhaps even to discover all of them. Even those with only limited exposure to electromagnetic concepts will find this book engrossing—and understandable. Pictures and prose relate the histories of the efforts made to understand the mysteries of our universe. This is a book that belongs in the collections of scientists and star gazers alike. 256 pp., 133 illus.

**Paper $12.95**        **Hard $18.95**
**Book No. 2946**

*Prices subject to change without notice.

---

### Look for these and other TAB books at your local bookstore.

---

**TAB BOOKS Inc.**
**Blue Ridge Summit, PA 17294-0850**

---

**Send for FREE TAB Catalog describing over 1200 current titles in print.**
OR CALL TOLL-FREE TODAY: **1-800-233-1128**
IN PENNSYLVANIA AND ALASKA, CALL: **717-794-2191**